Junior Petkeeper's Library

FISH

Fiona Henrie

Consultant Editor
Michael Findlay M.R.C.V.S.

Photographs by Marc Henrie A.S.C.

Franklin Watts
London New York Sydney Toronto 1980

Franklin Watts Limited
12a Golden Square
London W1

© 1980 Franklin Watts Limited

Reprinted 1983

SBN UK edition: 85166 859 3
SBN US edition: 531 04184 0
Library of Congress Catalog Card No: 80 50481

Phototypeset by Tradespools Limited,
Frome, Somerset
Printed in Great Britain by
E. T. Heron, Essex

The publisher and author would like to thank the following
for their help in the preparation of this book:
All pets, Edgware; Jeremy Brown; Dr. D. M. Ford;
Queensborough Aquarium

Contents

If you become a responsible fish-keeper, or aquarist, you will have an interesting and absorbing hobby.

Introduction

Keeping fish can be very enjoyable. They are beautiful to look at, and it is fascinating to watch them swimming around. This book tells you how to look after freshwater fish.

At first you may need to buy expensive equipment, but afterwards fish cost very little to feed and look after. You must have your parents' permission to keep fish as you will need their help.

When you install the fish tank, some pieces of equipment need to be connected to the power supply. Never try to connect the equipment by yourself, because working with electricity can be dangerous.

Note to parents

If you decide to have a tank of fish in your home, please be absolutely sure that it is wanted by your child and yourself, and that the interest will not wear off after the first few weeks.

You must be sure that you are willing to supervise the installation, care and well-being of the fish.

You will also need to bear the cost of the initial outlay, which can be expensive, and the upkeep, which is minimal.

It would be unfair to your child and your family to become unwilling pet keepers.

A shop which specializes in fish will have many different kinds of fish in stock.

Talk to the shopkeeper if you are not sure which fish to choose. The shopkeeper will also be able to advise you on the best plants, food or equipment to buy.

Choosing fish

You may know someone who has bred fish successfully and has some for sale.

If you go to a pet shop or store which specializes in fish, there will be a large selection to choose from. Make sure you buy your fish from a store that has a good reputation for healthy stock.

When you choose different kinds of fish for your tank, check with the shopkeeper that they are able to live together. A large or aggressive fish will bully—or even eat—smaller fish. A tank which holds different varieties of fish is called a community tank.

A healthy fish, like the angel fish should be able to swim easily and have an undamaged body. Check that the fish you choose are free of disease.

Be sure that the fish you choose are healthy. Disease will spread very quickly from one fish to the others.

The fish should be able to swim freely and easily. There should not be any cuts or wounds on their bodies, or any split or damaged fins. Check that there are no tiny white spots or fluffy patches on their bodies or fins.

The eyes should be clear and lie flat on the head. Do not buy a fish with protruding or sunken eyes.

The shades of a healthy fish will be strong and bright, while those of a sick or disturbed fish will fade.

7

Sunset platys are fish which give birth to live young.

Varieties of fish

Get as much variety as possible in your tank: fish like tetras, angel fish and black mollies provide contrast in shape and shade. Buy a catfish to clean the bottom of the tank.

Choose fish which live at different levels. Their shapes often vary. Most surface-swimmers have flat backs and curved undersides. Fish which swim in the middle of the tank are evenly curved above and below. Many fish which live on the bottom have curved backs and flat undersides.

8

The following are all good fresh-water community fish—guppies, mollies, sword tails and platys are fish which give birth to live young.

Other fish lay eggs. These include the tetras, black widows, pencil fish, penguin fish, catfish, gouramis, angel fish, zebra danios, tiger barbs and Siamese fighting fish (buy one of these only as these fish will fight with each other).

If you keep cold-water fish, you can include the common goldfish, fancy goldfish, koi carp and shubunkin.

All angel fish, like the black marbled variety above, lay eggs.

Gouramis are egg-laying fish.

9

The tank

The size of the tank you choose will depend on the number of fish you want to keep. Fish breathe oxygen which enters through the surface of the water. Allow 930 sq. cm (12 sq. in) of surface water for each 2.5 cm (1 in) of fish. To find out the water surface of the tank, multiply the length of the tank by the width.

It is very important that the tank is large enough for the number of fish you are going to keep. A tank 60 × 38 × 30 cm (24 × 15 × 12 in) in size will comfortably hold about fifteen tropical fish up to 5 cm (2 in) long.

Check that the tank is strong and leakproof. There must not be any broken joints.

The tank will need a cover which is raised slightly to allow air to pass underneath. The cover keeps dust out of the tank and stops lively fish from jumping out. It also holds the lighting unit.

10

A tank filled with water is very heavy. Decide where you want to put the tank before you install it. See that the table, shelf or stand on which you put the tank is strong enough to take the weight.

Do not put the tank near a window where direct sunlight will shine through the sides of the tank. It is better for the fish to have the light coming from above as it would in their natural surroundings. You can put an artificial light in the cover.

Put the tank near an electric outlet so that you do not have electric wires trailing across your floor.

Above left
Choose the place for your tank before you begin to fill it up. You can buy a special stand on which to put the tank.

Above right
You can keep fish even if you have other pets at home – but always make sure that the tank is covered!

11

Gravel comes in a wide variety of bright shades, as well as in natural stone shades.

Box filter which goes on top of the gravel. A box filter can also be placed outside the tank.

Equipment for the tank

You will need some gravel for the bottom of the tank. You can buy gravel in natural stone shades or in very bright shades.

If you keep a number of fish, buy an air pump and filter to keep the water fresh. Air lines, made of plastic tubing, connect the pump to the filter.

There are two kinds of filters. One goes on top of the gravel. This filter is a plastic box filled with synthetic wool and charcoal. It is easy to change the wool when it becomes dirty.

The other type of filter goes beneath

12

Before you put the gravel in the tank, wash the gravel thoroughly in cold water. Dirt or grit left in the gravel will make the tank water look cloudy.

Place an under-gravel filter in the tank before putting anything else in. On the left-hand side of the tank is a slim, strip thermometer.

Heater and thermostat fitted together in one unit.

the gravel. Many people like to use an under-gravel filter because it cannot be seen. However, you cannot clean it without dismantling the tank.

If you keep tropical fish, you will need a water heater and a thermostat. You can buy these separately or in one unit. The thermostat controls the heater, and so keeps the water at the correct temperature.

Buy a thermometer to check the temperature of the water. Some thermometers float in the water, while others can be attached to the side of the tank.

13

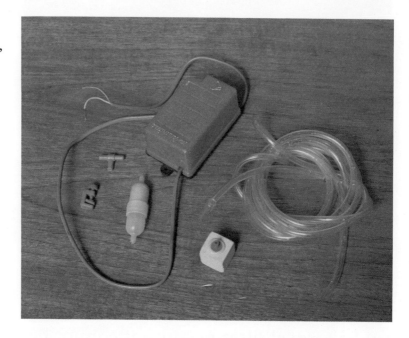

This picture shows a pump and the plastic air lines, with the various connecting parts.

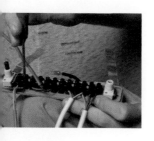

Use a cable holder to keep all the wires neat.

Connecting the electrical equipment

Place the pump at the back of the tank and attach the air lines to it. Connect the air lines to the filter. Put the heater and the thermostat at the back of the tank, too.

With the help of an adult, connect the different pieces of electrical equipment to the power source. Do not connect the equipment by yourself.

All electrical connections must be made outside the tank. Insulate the

14

The tank cover holds the lighting unit. A fluorescent tube is best as it will not overheat the water. If you like, you can connect the light to a time switch so that it turns on and off automatically. All the other electrical equipment must stay on all the time.

wires with waterproof tape to protect them from getting wet. Use a cable holder to keep the wires neat.

Put a fluorescent tube into the cover of the tank. Fluorescent light is not hot so it will not overheat the water. A fluorescent light also lasts longer than an ordinary light bulb and uses less electricity.

Switch on the power to check that the equipment is working, and then switch it off until you have filled the tank with water.

Use waterproof insulating tape to protect the wires from water. It is very dangerous to let water get on open electrical equipment.

Filling the tank with water

Use a pail or hose to fill two-thirds of the tank with cold water. Hold a saucer at an angle and pour the water onto it. This prevents the gravel from being disturbed. Most tap water is chlorinated, so put some de-chlorinator in the water as chlorine is harmful to fish.

Put the plants in now and continue to fill the tank until the water reaches about 1 cm ($\frac{1}{2}$ in) from the top. Put tap water conditioner in the water.

Switch on the electrical equipment and check that everything is working properly. Let the water reach a temperature of about 24 °C (75 °F) before you put the fish in.

16

Common goldfish in a cold-water tank. Notice how the red gravel brightens up the tank. Do not keep goldfish with tropical fish as goldfish need to be kept in cooler water.

Cold-water fish

Fish such as goldfish can be kept in cold-water tanks. You will not need to buy a heater or thermostat. The best temperature for cold-water fish is about 15 °C (60 °F). Check that the water does not get too warm during hot weather.

A tank 60 × 38 × 30 cm (24 × 15 × 12 in) in size is large enough for four goldfish 7.5 cm (3 in) long. Put in gravel, rocks, plants, filter, pump and lighting as with a heated tank.

All fish need space and places where they can shelter. If you are given a goldfish, or win one at a fair, it is unkind to put it into a small bowl with nothing except water in it.

Comet goldfish in a tank. Set up the tank in the same way as for tropical fish, but without the heater. Do not let the water get too warm in a heated room in winter, or during hot weather in summer.

17

Plants

Plants are an important addition to the tank. They provide shelter for the fish and help to keep the water fresh. Plants also add oxygen to the water.

There are many different kinds of plants. Start with plants like elodea or vallisneria, which grow quickly. Put the plants in water until you need to put them into the tank. You can plant directly into the gravel, but plants will be easier to position if you put them in pots of peat which are buried beneath the gravel.

A selection of water plants. They include, from left to right: myrio, rotala, water wisteria, Amazon sword, wheat plant, red ivy, hygrophilia and vallisneria.

You can buy plastic plants as well as live ones. All the plants in this tank are made of plastic.

18

When you put the plants in the tank, make sure the roots go straight down. Use a planting stick so that you do not damage the plants with your fingers.

Keep the plants at the back third of the tank. This leaves the front of the tank free for you to see the fish. Add plant food to the water to help the plants establish themselves.

Use special plant food to feed the plants every two to four weeks, depending on how many there are in the tank.

A planting stick is very useful for putting plants in the tank.

Peat provides food for the plants. You can use pots of peat or peat granules. Put the granules under the gravel at the back third of the tank where the plants will be.

19

When the shopkeeper packs up the fish, some oxygen is trapped at the top of the bag.

If the bag of fish is large, the shopkeeper may add oxygen from a cylinder.

Fish arrive at shops in polystyrene boxes. The boxes protect the fish from the heat and cold.

Buying fish

When you choose your fish, the shopkeeper will put them in a plastic bag with some of the water from the shop's tank.

The shopkeeper will close the bag tightly, trapping some air in the space above the water. Some shopkeepers fill this space with oxygen from a cylinder.

In hot weather put the fish into a shopping bag to keep out the light and to prevent the water from getting too warm. If the weather is cold, wrap the plastic bag in a sweater to keep the correct water temperature. If you let the water get too cold, it may harm the fish.

20

Never put new fish straight into the tank. Let the closed bag float in the tank until the temperature of the water in the bag is the same as the temperature of the water in the tank. To transfer the fish, empty the contents of the bag into a net held over a container. Then put the netted fish into a tank.

Putting fish into the tank

When you get home, float the closed plastic bag in the tank water.

Leave the bag for about ten to twenty minutes and then open it gently. Check the temperatures of the water inside the bag and the water inside the tank. When they are the same, use a net to transfer the fish to the tank.

Begin with a few fish. When they have settled in, add a few more. Buy fish in threes—two females and one male. Buy only one catfish. One catfish will help keep the tank clean. If you have more than one, they may start eating the plants.

Buy a catfish for your tank as it will help keep the tank clean.

21

Fish need very little food. A pinch of food flakes is usually enough. Add a little more only if the fish seem to want it. Overfeeding is a common cause of death. Feed your fish six days a week and let them go without food for one day.

You can buy fish flakes in cans or packets. This picture shows a can of goldfish flakes.

Feeding

Fish need to eat special food which you can buy from a pet shop. You can buy a variety of fish flakes. Some flakes are made from dried cereal, but the best are made from fresh food.

Sprinkle the flakes on the surface of the water. If the fish eat it up and seem to be looking for more, put in another pinch. After a few minutes remove all uneaten flakes from the water.

Some fish come to the top of the tank to feed, while others remain in the middle or the bottom of the tank. Make sure some of the food reaches those fish which do not feed at the top.

22

Floating dispenser for daphnia. As the daphnia float out of the dispenser the fish eat them up.

Feed the fish once or twice a day as they need to be fed small amounts regularly. However, it is easy to overfeed fish, so only give as much as they can eat in three or four minutes.

Give your fish some live food from time to time. You can buy daphnia (water fleas) or tubifex (minute blood worms) from a pet shop. The shopkeeper will put the live food with its water in a plastic bag.

Put the daphnia in a special dispenser which floats at the top of the tank. Release some of the daphnia for the middle and bottom feeders. Drop the tubifex straight into the tank.

Breeding

Some fish lay eggs. Other fish give birth to live young. These fish are called live-bearers.

It is easy to tell the difference between male and female live-bearers. When the male's anal fin (or gonopodium) matures, it changes shape. It becomes longer and thinner. The gonopodium holds the sperm used to fertilize the eggs.

The body of a female live-bearer becomes fat and bulging when she has eggs inside her. The male fertilizes the eggs while they are inside the

24

female. The eggs grow inside the female until it is time for the fry (young fish) to be born.

Male and female egg-layers are difficult to tell apart. Sometimes the male is larger, or varies in shade.

The female lays eggs which are immediately fertilized by the male. The fertilized eggs develop in the water until it is time for them to be hatched. Hatching times vary from fish to fish.

Some fish lay their eggs among the gravel and plants. They may leave the eggs to hatch by themselves or stay to look after them.

Although a breeding tank does not need to be as large as the community tank, you will need to fit it up with the same equipment. Separate the adult fish if they start eating the young. Put the large fish back into the community tank, or put the young into a third, nursery tank if you want the adult fish to continue breeding.

Breeding fish in tanks can be very difficult. Fish will only breed if they feel "at home" in the tank. You may be able to encourage breeding, though. Add a jugful of warm water so that the temperature rises to about 26 °C (79 °F).

When breeding fish, use a separate breeding tank because the adult fish may eat the eggs or the fry.

Put a breeding trap inside the tank. The trap has small holes through which only the young can swim. Put the young in the main tank when they are large enough not to be eaten. At first, feed the young on powdered dry food, brine shrimp and sifted daphnia.

26

Use a small net to catch dead leaves and left-over food. When you want to catch fish, use two nets. This makes catching fish easier for you and less disturbing for the fish.

Cleaning the tank

Each week remove about a fifth of the water in the tank. Put in fresh tap water which has been standing for a day. Add some tap water conditioner and de-chlorinator to the new water. Check its temperature before putting it into the tank.

Clean the glass every week. You can use a special scraper for this job.

Remove dead leaves and uneaten food every day. Whenever necessary, clean the inside of the glass. You can use a special scraper for cleaning the glass.

Keep your tank free of algae. Algae are very small, simple green plants. Too much algae will make the tank water look green.

Before you put new plants in the tank, wash them in salt water. The salt water helps to remove germs. Rinse the plants carefully in fresh water before you put them in the tank.

Health care

If you keep your tank clean and do not overcrowd it, the fish will be healthy and less likely to catch diseases.

Disease may be introduced to a healthy tank when you buy new plants or fish. Wash new plants in salt water before putting them into the tank. Do not put new fish into the tank until you are sure they are completely healthy.

The two most common diseases are white spot and fungus. White spot produces tiny white spots on the fish's body or fins. Each spot is smaller than

28

a pinhead. Fungus looks like patches of fluff. You can buy medicine for both these diseases at the pet shop. Follow the instructions on the packet carefully.

For some diseases, like fin rot (which causes the fins to rot within a few days), infected wounds and boils, you will need veterinary care. Contact your vet, who will prescribe special treatment. Fish can catch tuberculosis or may have a growth. These illnesses cannot be treated. If a fish cannot swim properly or feed itself through illness, it is kinder to end its life humanely.

If you think a fish has a disease which the other fish could catch easily, you can put it in a small tank by itself. If a fish has a disease which cannot be treated, do not let it suffer unnecessarily.

29

Checklist

Before you get your fish

● Buy a tank, filter, air pump, heater and thermostat (for tropical fish only), gravel, rocks, plants, electrical attachments, tap-water conditioner, de-chlorinator, food

Each day

● Feed the fish once or twice a day
● Remove uneaten food and debris from the tank
● Check that the fish are healthy and are eating properly

Each week

● Change about a fifth of the water
● Check that the tank is free of algae
● Check that the equipment is working properly

When necessary

● Consult the vet
● Treat the fish for illness
● If you have a filter which goes on top of the gravel, change the filter material when it looks dirty

Glossary

Algae — simple green plants which grow in water.

Community tank — tank which houses a variety of fish which live well together.

Daphnia — water fleas.

Egg-layer — fish which lays eggs.

Fresh water — water which is not salty.

Fry — young fish.

Gono-podium — anal fin of male live-bearer which produces sperm.

Live-bearer — fish which gives birth to live young.

Mucus — protective covering on a fish's body and fins.

Tropical fish — fish from warm climates. These fish must be kept in heated tanks.

Tubifex — minute blood worms.

Index